Pat Croce's

VICTORY JOURNAL

Pat Croce's

VICTORY JOURNAL

A Daily Diary *for* Success *and* Celebration

RUNNING PRESS
PHILADELPHIA · LONDON

9 8 7 6 5 4 3 2 1
Digit on the right indicates the number of this printing

ISBN 0-7624-1594-0

Designed by Matt Goodman
Edited by Greg Jones

This book may be ordered by mail from the publisher.
Please include $2.50 for postage and handling.
But try your bookstore first!

Running Press Book Publishers
125 South Twenty-second Street
Philadelphia, Pennsylvania 19103-4399

Visit Pat Croce on the web!
www.Ifeelgreat.com

Visit us on the web!
www.runningpress.com

INTRODUCTION

There are many tools available that help monitor your journey through life. Things like daily planners and diaries, report cards, and performance appraisals.

But let me suggest something new: a *Victory Journal.*

Like many professionals, I wouldn't think of starting my day without glancing at my day planner, reviewing my to-do list, and calculating the achievement of my daily game plan. But unlike most individuals, I supplement this preview with an end-of-the-day *review* that makes all that work worthwhile. I call this my "Victory Journal," and I write in it every night.

The content of any *Victory Journal* should include a wide range of topics. One page may feature exultant notes about the culmination of a huge deal; another may simply contain a few giddy words about a great workout with a friend in need of shedding some stress.

Feel free to record pleasant surprises, the receipt of thank-you letters and pats on the back, the sharing of acts of kindness and words of wisdom, and *anything* at all that demonstrates your power to have a positive impact on the day.

Obviously, some victories are very subjective. And other victories are definitely objective. But as long as you perceive something to be a victory (and we all know that perception is reality), then it *is* a victory and it deserves a place in your *Victory Journal.*

Like a photo album, your *Victory Journal* will become a great collection of snapshots of positive experiences and a living reminder of your power to achieve. With such a clear record of all your daily wins, successes, achievements, and celebrations, you will slowly build a strong foundation for success.

The *Victory Journal* can be especially useful when your "thinkin' becomes stinkin'" and your attitude has twisted and soured. Any committed optimist worth his weight in wisdom would admit that it's difficult to remain upbeat and positive when the critics and cynics are forecasting rain on your parade. In such times, one glance at the pages of your *Victory Journal* can be quite restorative. You quickly see that you *have been* a winner and realize that you *can be* a winner again. Success begets success, and the simple act of reading your *Victory Journal* should prepare you to make another journal entry!

Best of all, your *Victory Journal* entries can be anything from just a few keywords or simple sentences to a page-long overview of a particular achievement. The idea is to stimulate a mental reproduction of those special snapshots of success, which you can recall and savor for the rest of your life.

—Pat Croce

THE WORLD NEEDS ALL THE HELP YOU CAN GIVE BY WAY OF CHEERFUL,

OPTIMISTIC, INSPIRING THOUGHT AND PERSONAL EXAMPLE.

—Grenville Kleiser

AT THE CENTER OF THE UNIVERSE IS A LOVING HEART THAT CONTINUES TO BEAT AND THAT WANTS THE BEST FOR

EVERY PERSON. ANYTHING WE CAN DO TO HELP FOSTER THE INTELLECT AND SPIRIT AND GROWTH

OF OUR FELLOW HUMAN BEINGS, THAT IS OUR JOB. THOSE OF US WHO HAVE THIS

PARTICULAR VISION MUST CONTINUE AGAINST ALL ODDS.

—Fred Rogers

Personal gain is empty if you do not feel you

have positively touched another's life.

—*Barbara Walters*

Give the world the best that you have,

and the best will come back to you.

—*Madeline Bridges*

If you haven't got any charity in your heart, you

have the worst kind of heart trouble.

—Bob Hope

Instead of spreading and embellishing the word about someone's misfortune

and misdeeds, try trumpeting triumphs and successes.

—Pat Croce

TO LAUGH OFTEN AND MUCH; TO WIN THE RESPECT OF INTELLIGENT PEOPLE AND AFFECTION OF CHILDREN; TO EARN THE

APPRECIATION OF HONEST CRITICS AND ENDURE THE BETRAYAL OF FALSE FRIENDS; TO APPRECIATE BEAUTY; TO FIND

THE BEST IN OTHERS; TO LEAVE THE WORLD A BIT BETTER, WHETHER BY A HEALTHY CHILD, A GARDEN PATCH

OR A REDEEMED SOCIAL CONDITION; TO KNOW EVEN ONE LIFE HAS BREATHED EASIER BECAUSE

YOU HAVE LIVED. THIS IS TO HAVE SUCCEEDED.

—Ralph Waldo Emerson

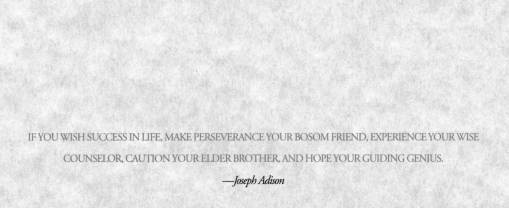

IF YOU WISH SUCCESS IN LIFE, MAKE PERSEVERANCE YOUR BOSOM FRIEND, EXPERIENCE YOUR WISE

COUNSELOR, CAUTION YOUR ELDER BROTHER, AND HOPE YOUR GUIDING GENIUS.

—Joseph Adison

Eighty percent of success is showing up.

—*Woody Allen*

My mother drew a distinction between achievement and success. She said that achievement is the knowledge that you have studied and done the best that or achievement and forget about success.

—*Helen Hayes*

When you allow yourself to feel great because someone else has succeeded, you end up feeling better about yourself.

—Pat Croce

Strength does not come from physical capacity.

It comes from an indomitable will.

—Mahatma Gandhi

THE DIFFERENCE BETWEEN A SUCCESSFUL PERSON AND OTHERS IS NOT A LACK OF
STRENGTH, NOT A LACK OF KNOWLEDGE, BUT RATHER A LACK OF WILL.

—*Vince Lombardi*

YOU WILL BE AS SMALL AS YOUR CONTROLLING DESIRE;

AS GREAT AS YOUR DOMINANT ASPIRATION.

—*James Allen*

What lies behind us and what lies before us are
small compared to what lies within us.

—*Ralph Waldo Emerson*

Everyone has talent. What is rare is the courage to follow

that talent to the dark place where it leads.

—*Erica Jong*

The will is an incredible resource of power that exists inside everyone—if you apply it,
you can change your life. I've seen it work too many times not to believe.
—Pat Croce

Success is measured not so much by the position that one has reached in life
as by the obstacles which he has overcome while trying to succeed.
—Booker T. Washington

IT IS NOT THE MOUNTAIN WE CONQUER, BUT OURSELVES.

—*Sir Edmund Hillary*

YOU GAIN STRENGTH, COURAGE AND CONFIDENCE BY EVERY EXPERIENCE IN WHICH YOU REALLY STOP TO LOOK FEAR IN

THE FACE. YOU ARE ABLE TO SAY TO YOURSELF, "I LIVED THROUGH THIS HORROR. I CAN TAKE THE NEXT

THING THAT COMES ALONG." YOU MUST DO THE THING YOU THINK YOU CANNOT DO.

—Eleanor Roosevelt

Impossible dreams are achieved one goal at a time.

—*Herman Cain*

Good timber does not grow with ease;

the stronger the wind, the stronger the trees.

—*J. Willard Marriott*

Look into the mirror and do a careful assessment. . . . Search for the good qualities and important experiences that those laugh lines on your face signify . . . the joyful moments, the hard-won victories.

—Pat Croce

The best mind-altering drug is truth.

—Lily Tomlin

DON'T COMPROMISE YOURSELF. YOU ARE ALL YOU GOT.

—Janis Joplin

HONESTY IS THE SINGLE MOST IMPORTANT FACTOR HAVING A DIRECT BEARING ON

THE FINAL SUCCESS OF AN INDIVIDUAL, CORPORATION, OR PRODUCT.

—Ed McMahon

Peace will come wherever it is sincerely invited. Love will overflow every sanctuary given it.
Truth will grow where the fertilizer that nourishes it is also truth.

—Alice Walker

Meditate. Don't think of all that you have to do, think of all that you have already accomplished. Meditation is like the one-minute rest between rounds in boxing. Give yourself a break from the pummeling of the daily grind.

—Pat Croce

I have had a lot of success with failure.

—*Thomas Edison*

The greatest glory in living lies not in never falling,

but in rising every time we fall.

—*Nelson Mandela*

ONLY THOSE WHO DARE TO FAIL GREATLY CAN EVER ACHIEVE GREATLY.

—*Robert F. Kennedy*

If you don't quit, and don't cheat, and don't run home

when trouble arrives, then you can only win.

—Shelly Long

I've had some ideas that worked, and even a few that worked really well. And I've had a thousand cockamamie ideas that were flaming failures and deserved to be. But I never gave up. You can't ever give up.

—Pat Croce

THE ROAD TO CONFIDENCE

IS PAVED WITH LITTLE VICTORIES.

—Anonymous

WE CAN DO NO GREAT THINGS

—ONLY SMALL THINGS WITH GREAT LOVE.

—*Mother Theresa*

Value is in the doer, not the deed.

—*Dennis Waitley*

There are glimpses of heaven to us in every act, or thought,

or word that raises us above ourselves.

—*Arthur P. Stanley*

It is the greatest of all mistakes to do nothing because
you can do only a little. Do what you can.
—Sydney Smith

Miracles come in all shapes and sizes . . . if you spend all your time waiting for super nova miracles,

you'll overlook all the small ones that happen all around you every single day.

—Pat Croce

THE WAY TO BE NOTHING IS TO DO NOTHING.

—*Nathaniel Howe*

AS YOU GROW OLDER YOU WILL DISCOVER THAT YOU HAVE TWO HANDS.

ONE IS FOR HELPING YOURSELF, THE OTHER FOR HELPING OTHERS.

—Audrey Hepburn

You cannot do a kindness too soon for you

never know when it will be too late.

—*Ralph Waldo Emerson*

A kind and compassionate act is often its own reward.

—*William J. Bennett*

The human spirit is not measured by the size of the act, but by the size of the heart.

—Memorial banner at Ground Zero

Perform random acts of kindness. . . . The opportunities are all around you.

You are going to be amazed at how good you will feel.

—Pat Croce

DO WHAT YOU CAN TO SHOW YOU CARE ABOUT OTHER PEOPLE,

AND YOU WILL MAKE OUR WORLD A BETTER PLACE.

—Rosalynn Carter

BE KIND AND MERCIFUL. LET NO ONE EVER COME TO YOU

WITHOUT COMING AWAY BETTER AND HAPPIER.

—*Mother Theresa*

When we seek to discover the best in others, we

somehow bring out the best in ourselves.

—*William Arthur Ward*

No act of kindness, however small, is ever wasted.

—*Aesop*

You will find as you look back upon your life that the moments when you have truly lived are the moments when you have done things in the spirit of love.

—Henry Drummond

There is always something to be gained from watching a victorious moment. . . . It gives you both

an appreciation and inspiration of what can be accomplished by the human spirit.

—Pat Croce

LIFE IS EITHER A DARING ADVENTURE OR NOTHING.

—*Helen Keller*

I HAVE A FRIEND WHO LIVES BY A THREE-WORD PHILOSOPHY: "SEIZE THE MOMENT."

JUST POSSIBLY, SHE MAY BE THE WISEST WOMAN ON THE PLANET.

—*Erma Bombeck*

Some of us are timid. We think we have something
to lose so we don't try for the next hill.

—*Maya Angelou*

Twenty years from now you will be more disappointed by the things you didn't do than by the ones you did do. So throw off the bowlines. Sail away from the safe harbor. Catch the trade winds in your sails. Explore. Dream. Discover.

—*Mark Twain*

You only live once, but if you do
it right, once is enough.
—Mae West

There was an elderly man who continued to run in marathons despite his advanced age, and when he was asked how he could keep up such a pace, he smiled and replied, "I tell lies to my legs."

Terrific concept, mind over matter. If you don't mind, then it doesn't matter.

—Pat Croce

NOTHING SHOULD BE PRIZED MORE HIGHLY

THAN THE VALUE OF EACH DAY.

—*Goethe*

LIFE ISN'T ABOUT FINDING YOURSELF.

LIFE IS ABOUT CREATING YOURSELF.

—*George Bernard Shaw*

Life itself is the proper binge.

—*Julia Child*

Life never becomes a habit to me.

It's always a marvel.

—*Katherine Mansfield*

You will do foolish things,
but do them with enthusiasm.

—Colette

Have faith. Give yourself over to the master plan. Faith has been described, in high-jump terms,

as nothing more than throwing your heart over the bar—and letting your body follow.

—Pat Croce

CHALLENGES MAKE YOU DISCOVER THINGS ABOUT YOURSELF THAT YOU NEVER REALLY KNEW. THEY'RE

WHAT MAKE THE INSTRUMENT STRETCH, WHAT MAKE YOU GO BEYOND THE NORM.

—*Cicely Tyson*

TO SEEK VISIONS, TO DREAM DREAMS, IS ESSENTIAL, AND IT IS ALSO ESSENTIAL TO TRY NEW WAYS OF LIVING,

TO MAKE ROOM FOR SERIOUS EXPERIMENTATION, TO RESPECT THE EFFORT EVEN WHERE IT FAILS.

—*Adrienne Rich*

To succeed, jump at opportunities as

quickly as you do at conclusions.

—Benjamin Franklin

The greater danger for most of us lies not in setting our aim too high and falling short;

but in setting our aim too low, and achieving our mark.

—*Michelangelo*

If we did all the things we are capable of,

we would literally astound ourselves.

—Thomas Edison

Bring order to your junk drawer…This can all be very symbolic—your junk drawer brought under control today can be your life being brought under control tomorrow…you will feel so proud, so utterly organized, so very much in charge.

—Pat Croce

I CAN LIVE TWO MONTHS ON A GOOD COMPLIMENT.

—*Mark Twain*

GIVE YOURSELF A PAT ON THE BACK EACH TIME YOU

HANG IN THERE WHEN YOU'VE SCORED.

—Marilyn C. Barrick

Flatter me, and I may not believe you. Criticize me, and I may not like you. Ignore me, and I may not forgive you. Encourage me, and I may not forget you.
—William Arthur

Take a moment to indulge in some self-congratulation when you've reached a goal. Savor the little triumphs, the small achievements. Self-praise is a nice way to remind yourself that you're making progress, inch-by-foot-by-yard-by-mile.

—Pat Croce

ACT AS IF IT WERE IMPOSSIBLE TO FAIL.

—*Dorothea Brande*

NOTHING IS MORE IMPORTANT TO THE FUTURE OF AN IDEA

THAN THE FIRST STEP YOU TAKE TO TRY IT OUT.

—*O. A. Battista*

Life is not meant to be easy, my child; but

take courage—it can be delightful.

—*George Bernard Shaw*

We do not choose our historical epoch, the country of our birth, or the immediate circumstances of our upbringing.

We do not, most of us, choose to die; nor do we choose the time and conditions of our death.

But within this realm of choicelessness, we do choose how we live.

—Joseph Epstein

WE MUST COMBINE THE TOUGHNESS OF THE SERPENT AND THE SOFTNESS

OF THE DOVE, A TOUGH MIND AND A TENDER HEART.

—*Martin Luther King, Jr.*

LIFE IS A COMPROMISE OF WHAT YOUR EGO WANTS TO DO, WHAT EXPERIENCE

TELLS YOU TO DO, AND WHAT YOUR NERVES LET YOU DO.

—*Bruce Crampton*

There are only two things really worth worrying about—either you're sick or you're well…either you get well or you die.

If you die…either you go to heaven or to hell. If you go to heaven, there's nothing to worry about. If you

go to hell, you'll be so busy partying with all your friends there will be nothing to worry about!

—Pat Croce

A rock pile ceases to be a rock pile the moment a single man contemplates it, bearing within him the image of a cathedral.

—Antoine De Saint-Exupury

We are what we repeatedly do.

Excellence, then, is not an act, but a habit.

—Aristotle

We are still masters of our fate.

We are still captains of our souls.

—Winston Churchill

GRAIN BY GRAIN – A LOAF; STONE

UPON STONE—A PALACE.

—*George Bernard Shaw*

NOTHING IN THE WORLD CAN TAKE THE PLACE OF PERSISTENCE. TALENT WILL NOT; NOTHING IN THE WORLD IS MORE COMMON THAN UNSUCCESSFUL MEN WITH TALENT. GENIUS WILL NOT; UNREWARDED GENIUS IS A PROVERB. EDUCATION WILL NOT; THE WORLD IS FULL OF EDUCATED DERELICTS. PERSISTENCE AND DETERMINATION ALONE ARE OMNIPOTENT.

—Calvin Coolidge

I once heard that your life is not measured by the number of breaths you take, but by the number of moments that take your breath away. And I want to increase that number.

—Pat Croce

ABOUT THE AUTHOR

Pat Croce, author of the *New York Times* bestseller *I Feel Great and You Will Too!* (Running Press) and the inspirational *110%* (Running Press), is the minority owner and former president of the Philadelphia 76ers, founder of Sports Physical Therapists, Inc., an international karate champion, a sought-after motivational speaker, and a dedicated family man. He and his wife, Diane, reside in suburban Philadelphia with their two children.